First Métis Man of Odesa

Also by Matthew MacKenzie

Bears
After the Fire & The Particulars

First
Métis Man
of Odesa

Matthew MacKenzie
& Mariya Khomutova

Playwrights Canada Press
Toronto

LIBRARY AND ARCHIVES CANADA CATALOGUING IN PUBLICATION
Title: First Métis man of Odesa / Matthew MacKenzie & Mariya Khomutova.
Names: MacKenzie, Matthew, author | Khomutova, Mariya, author.
Identifiers: Canadiana (print) 20240416708 | Canadiana (ebook) 20240416732
  | ISBN 9780369105127 (softcover) | ISBN 9780369105134 (PDF)
  | ISBN 9780369105141 (EPUB)
Subjects: LCGFT: Drama.
Classification: LCC PS8625.K454 F57 2024 | DDC c812/.6—dc23

Playwrights Canada Press staff work across Turtle Island, on Treaty 7, Treaty 13, and Treaty 20 territories, which are the current and ancestral homes of the Anishinaabe Nations (Ojibwe / Chippewa, Odawa, Potawatomi, Algonquin, Saulteaux, Nipissing, and Mississauga / Michi Saagiig), the Blackfoot Confederacy (Kainai, Piikani, and Siksika), néhiyaw, Sioux, Stoney Nakoda, Tsuut'ina, Wendat, and members of the Haudenosaunee Confederacy (Mohawk, Oneida, Onondaga, Cayuga, Seneca, and Tuscarora), as well as Metis and Inuit peoples. It always was and always will be Indigenous land.

We acknowledge the financial support of the Canada Council for the Arts, the Ontario Arts Council (OAC), Ontario Creates, the Government of Ontario, and the Government of Canada for our publishing activities.

For the first Métis man of Odesa, Ivan.

Foreword
Lianna Makuch

This is a love story. And like any grand, sweeping love story, our lovers are faced with grand, sweeping obstacles that challenge their fate. They are faced with modern challenges like Facebook messaging over great distances throughout a pandemic. And like the many great love stories that came before them, Matt and Masha's story is also set against the backdrop of war.

I have been witness to Matt and Masha's love story from the beginning. It is only fitting that these two theatrical romantics would fatefully meet through the theatre. It was at a workshop of my play *Barvinok* in Kyiv that Matt and Masha first met in 2018. Matt was my dramaturg, and Mariya a workshop actor. The rest is history. It was another workshop of a new play of mine titled *Alina* that brought Matt back to Ukraine in 2020 prior to the pandemic. At the time, I had no idea that being their third wheel would grant me a unique perspective as the future director of *First Métis Man of Odesa*. I also had no idea exactly how quickly and significantly our worlds would change in so many ways just a few short years later.

When Russia's full-scale invasion of Ukraine began on February 24, 2022, it was impossible to turn away. For so many people part of the Ukrainian diaspora, the war was and continues to be omnipresent. Mundane, routine tasks are weighted. News about it is inescapable. The cognitive dissonance of scrolling through Instagram memes followed by images of horrific Russian war crimes is an ongoing reality as the war rages on. To be part of the Ukrainian diaspora is to contend with your head and heart reeling for your loved ones in Ukraine, and striving to not fully dissociate from your safe, physical reality. As political pundits, hot takes, and ideological debates about Ukraine aim to dehumanize the ongoing events, it is more important than ever to return to stories that embrace our humanity.

This is also a love story about Ukraine. Just as Matt and Masha's love blossomed on the cobblestone streets of Kyiv, or the ultra-romantic promenades outside the iconic Odesa Opera Theatre, there is so much about Ukraine to fall in love with. Like any grand, sweeping love story, this one shows us that not even the greatest obstacles, like the evil forces of war, can taint true love. Matt and Masha's son, Ivan, is a reminder of this unbreakable spirit. Ivan is a beautiful union of two cultures whose love has created a symbol of the kind of future we are fighting for.

Слава Україні. Все буде Україна.

Lianna Makuch is a Ukrainian Canadian theatre artist. She has travelled to Ukraine to research and develop her plays Barvinok *and* Alina, *gaining awards and recognition from both the theatre and Ukrainian communities. Lianna's directorial debut,* First Métis Man of Odesa, *received a Dora Mavor Moore Award for Outstanding Direction and has been seen on stages nationwide. She is an avid Ukrainian activist and has been recognized as one of 50 Canadian Fellows of Ukraine by the UDonation International NGO, listed in* Edify Edmonton's *Top 40 Under 40, and her theatre work has been referenced in the House of Commons.*

First Métis Man of Odesa was first produced by Punctuate! Theatre in association with Western Canada Theatre at the Pavilion Theatre, Kamloops, from March 16–25, 2023, with the following cast and creative team:

Performers: Matthew MacKenzie and Mariya Khomutova

Director: Lianna Makuch
Set and Lighting Design: Daniela Masellis
Projection Design: Amelia Scott
Composer: Daraba
Sound Design: Aaron Macri
Choreographer: Krista Lin
Dramaturgy: Matt McGeachy
Stage Manager: Lore Green
Rehearsal Stage Manager: Kiidra Duhault
Production Manager and Technical Director: Trent Crosby
Design Consultant and Scenic Artist: Dawn Marie Marchand
Beadwork: Krista Leddy
Producers: Sheiny Satanove and Andy Cohen
Associate Producers: Alyson Dicey and desirée leverenz
Head Scenic Painter: Emily Randall
Painting: Amy Powell

The play went on to be produced by Punctuate! Theatre in association with The Theatre Centre at The Theatre Centre, Toronto, from March 30–April 8, 2023; Citadel Theatre, Edmonton, from April 22–May 13, 2023; The Cultch, Vancouver, from May 25–June 4, 2023; Persephone Theatre, Saskatoon, from October 17–29, 2023; the Royal Manitoba Theatre Centre, Winnipeg, from November 1–18, 2023; Talk is Free Theatre, Barrie, from February 22–March 2, 2024; Soulpepper Theatre, Toronto, from May 8–19, 2024; and the National Arts Centre, Ottawa, from September 18–28, 2024.

Characters

Masha: Mid-thirties, of Odesa, new mother
Matt: Early-forties, of the Métis Nation of Alberta,
new father

Setting

That liminal space between coming and going,
true love and heartbreak, war and peace.

Pre-show light. Enter MATT.

MATT: Hello, everybody, my name is Matthew MacKenzie and I'm Artistic Director of Punctuate! Theatre. I'm not an actor, but in this play—a true story—I perform the role of myself, Matt MacKenzie.

Punctuate! Theatre is proud to be based in amiskwacîwâskahikan, on the banks of the Kisiskâciwan River, the traditional stompin' grounds of the Cree, Dene, Blackfoot, Saulteaux Nakota Sioux, Stoney and Métis.

Before we begin, I'd like to direct your attention to the last page of this book, where you'll find a QR code that will take you to information about where you can make a donation to support the efforts of some of the Ukrainians you will hear about this evening. Sláva Ukrayíni!

MASHA: *(off)* Heróyam sláva!

MATT: Thanks, everyone.

Exit MATT.

MASHA in light as Yelena from Lianna Makuch's Barvinok.

MASHA: "I don't want your donations."

Pause.

"We have donations . . . clothes, toys, food. No. What do I need? Let me tell you. I need an apartment. Can you give me an apartment?"

MASHA waits for a reply. She shakes her head.

"People come here with their donations and they stare at us, like animals in a zoo."

MASHA stares at the audience.

"Have you come to stare at me too?"

Silence. A mortar whistles overhead—MASHA freezes, taking cover.

Enter MATT.

MATT: October 21, 2018. My Canadian theatre colleagues and I have been in eastern Ukraine, near the front line between Ukrainian troops and Russian-backed separatists, conducting interviews for a play with people caught up in a conflict much of the world has forgotten about.

MASHA unfreezes.

Our research culminates in a workshop with Ukrainian actors in Kyiv, where I meet Masha, an actor originally from Odesa.

MASHA: This woman you spoke with, she asked you for an apartment?

MATT: No—well, yes, she was asking like . . . the West.

MASHA: You were taking requests?

MATT: No, we were conducting interviews. This is something she said.

MASHA: To relay to the West.

MATT: To the Canadian public at large, I guess.

MASHA: I don't believe that's what she meant.

MATT: You can watch the tape. That's what she said.

Pause. MASHA shrugs.

MASHA: "I don't want your donations. I want an apartment, in the West."

MATT: No, that's not what she said.

MASHA: That's what you said she said.

MATT: She said what's written on the page, nothing more, nothing less.

MASHA: In Canada you have subtext?

MATT: Yes.

MASHA: It sounds like she's saying, "I don't want to answer your questions—Canada, fuck off."

MATT: Yes. Perhaps.

MASHA shrugs.

Masha scared the b'Jesus out of my Canadian colleagues and myself. She'd studied Stanislavsky's acting method with a master, who studied with a master, who studied with Stanislavsky himself. She was—

MASHA: Three handshakes away from Stanislavsky, as we say.

MATT: Which is like a piano player being three handshakes away from Mozart.

MASHA: Most men get into theatre so that they can listen to their own voice as much as possible. But not Matthew. During our whole workshop he just sits and listens.

MASHA slowly circles MATT.

I always believed that smart people don't talk a lot, so Matt is this mysterious, silent fellow with kind eyes and a big forehead.

MATT: Masha starts to linger on the steps of the theatre after rehearsals.

MASHA: Matt lingers, not the other way around.

MATT: We go out to interview Ukrainian veterans and I invite Masha to join us.

MASHA: The veterans are fiery boys. They speak about a future Russian invasion with total conviction. But like many Ukrainians, I don't want to listen.

MATT: The veterans are members of the Bob Marley Squad—a reggae-loving group of friends who formed during the Maidan Revolution in 2013.

MASHA: Being at home drove me crazy during Maidan—I was too afraid to go to the square, so I just volunteered at a church near my house, making borscht for the protesters. Not very interesting.

MATT: No way—the famous Babushka Borscht Brigades!

MASHA: I am no babushka, and there is nothing exciting about making borscht, believe me.

MATT: But you did your part to support the protesters, and they were victorious.

MASHA: Yes, they overthrew the government.

MATT: Which led Russia to send in little green men to occupy Crimea and arming separatists to try to seize the Donbas in the east.

MASHA: Listen, I'm not the best example of political consciousness—I had just started a relationship in 2014 when war broke out in the east—my new boyfriend and I went to a yoga retreat.

MATT: Okay, but you were in the majority—most Ukrainians didn't fight in 2014. And when it became clear that the Ukrainian military wasn't in a position to defend Ukrainian territory, volunteers like the Bob Marley Squad rushed to the front.

MASHA: These guys were just kids. When they got to the front, they didn't even have guns.

MATT: They stopped the advance.

MASHA: But at what cost?

MATT: At an incredible cost. But they were fighting for their future, for liberty—they were fighting against tyranny, for you and me.

> *MATT is beckoned by the veterans to play a drinking game.*

MASHA: *(to audience)* Over the course of the week, Matt's Canadian colleagues tell me about some of his peculiarities.

> *MATT takes a drink. MASHA and MATT's text overlaps.*

MATT: *(to veterans)* Yeah, there are a lot of Ukrainians in Canada—the city where I'm from is nicknamed Edmonchuck.

MATT takes a drink.

MASHA: He has never had a "normal" job because he can't stand authority.

MATT: Have you heard of Gretzky?

MASHA: For fifteen years he ran his own house-painting company.

MATT: Have you heard of BPs?

MASHA: He took ten years to write his first play.

MATT: It stands for Boston Pizza—it's a huge restaurant in Canada, originally started in Edmonton.

MASHA: Over the course of that decade it took him to write his first play—

MATT: I'm not sure why they didn't call it Edmonton Pizza. Boston's just more exotic I guess—

MASHA: —he rewrote the same scene three hundred times.

MATT: Have you heard this song?

MATT sings and performs the chicken dance polka.

MASHA: He gets a group of hardened veterans to perform the chicken dance.

MATT: (*laughing*) Yeah! Originally recorded in Edmonton.

MATT does a shot, then returns to MASHA. Overlap stops.

MASHA: So, why did you come on this adventure?

MATT: To see. To learn.

MASHA: Do you think that by telling the stories of those who are suffering that the West will be inspired to save Ukraine?

MATT: We don't think we'll save anyone, but we do believe more people need to be paying attention to what's happening in Ukraine.

MASHA: I'm not sure that writing a play based on the real words of real people can be art.

MATT: Reality can be art.

MASHA: But it's not "real" the moment you put a person's real words into an actor's mouth.

MATT: It's not "real" in a literal sense, but I think there is the potential power to communicate a deeper truth through performance.

MASHA: So, if I want to write a play about myself and the events that truly happened in my life, it will be art?

MATT: If you experience something remarkable enough, or terrible enough, sure.

MASHA: If I truly suffer enough?

MATT shakes his head.

MATT: More theatre needs to be about the here and now—if I've got to watch another urgent adaptation of a Shakespeare or Chekhov, I'm going to gouge out my own eyes.

MASHA: You cannot reduce Chekhov to some dusty old guy from history—Chekhov is a master, a meat trader—he deals with the meat of the soul.

MATT: I have never considered that writers are butchers of souls.

MASHA: All the great writers and poets search for truth.

MATT: That's why I write—I'm trying to make sense of what is happening in the world, and in my head and in my heart.

MASHA: You compare yourself to the masters.

MATT: No, I'm saying that when I don't write, I lose my mind. So writing for me, searching, as you say, is a necessary thing.

MASHA: And the classics for me are a necessary thing.

MATT: We both have needs.

Shift.

MASHA: On the night before our performance, Matthew makes an excuse to find me backstage.

MATT: I'm part of the team. I don't need an excuse to say "break a leg."

MASHA: In Ukraine we say, "I hope you don't get a single feather." As if you are speaking to a hunter.

MATT: I hope you don't get a single feather.

MASHA: Damn you.

MASHA applies powder.

MATT: . . .

MASHA: Will there be champagne after the performance?

MATT: . . . Not to my knowledge.

MASHA stops applying powder.

MASHA: A premiere without champagne is like a field without wheat in Ukraine.

MATT slowly nods. Shift. Applause. A champagne bottle pops. MASHA and MATT clink crystal glasses. MASHA takes a sip.

It's bad luck not to drink after toasting.

MATT: I can't. I'm allergic.

MASHA: To champagne.

MATT: And to wine, peanuts, horses, and all moulds and grasses.

MASHA: So, you bought the champagne just for me.

MATT nods.

It has been an honour to meet you.

MATT: The honour has been all mine.

MATT and MASHA stare at each other.

MASHA: We say goodbye.

MASHA clicks her heels and salutes. MATT salutes awkwardly back.

This will be the last time I see this peculiar man, I am certain.

A jet plane takes off—brief movement.

But to my amazement, not long after we part, Matthew begins a correspondence.

MATT: We'd established a friendship.

MASHA: Over many months, Matthew messages me from all across Canada—or, "Turtle Island," as he calls it.

MATT: Masha messages me from all over Ukraine and the former Eastern Bloc.

MASHA: Matthew travels like a circus boy.

MATT: Masha travels like a Red Sparrow—a Soviet spy.

MASHA: Matthew loves the mountains.

MATT: Masha loves the sea.

MASHA: Matthew is Métis.

MATT: Masha is a seventh-generation Odesan.

MASHA: Matthew is a seventh-generation Edmontonian.

MATT: Masha goes on solo pilgrimages to the final resting spots of her favourite poets, then recites their poetry graveside, rain or shine.

MASHA: Matthew experienced heartbreak in his twenties and didn't date again for two thousand days.

MATT: Masha wants to get married and have a family.

MASHA: Matthew has never really thought about having a family.

MATT: My life is too crazy.

MASHA: I worry that I'm falling for somebody who is a world away, but after a YEAR of corresponding, Matthew messages me . . .

MATT: "Hey!"

MATT deletes.

"Howdy."

MATT deletes.

"Was it just me . . . "

MATT deletes.

"Forgive me for asking, but was it just me, or was there a spark between you and I when we met last year in Kyiv?"

MASHA: "Certainly."

Beat.

"You conquered me."

MATT and MASHA turn to each other.

I caution we must not get swept away too quickly—I want this to be real, not a flight of fancy.

MATT: Masha flies to me.

Movement—a jet plane lands.

MASHA: Toronto is amazing.

MATT: I can't believe she thinks Toronto is amazing.

MASHA: I try venison for the first time!

MATT: Five hundred and fifty-three metres in the sky.

MASHA: We go to Niagara Falls!

MATT: Embracing in the mist—

MASHA: Like in the movie, with Marilyn Monroe!

MASHA expects a kiss, but MATT barges past.

MATT: We stop in Odessa, Ontario.

MASHA: It is nothing like the Odesa I know.

MATT: We go to La Belle Province and climb the mountain in Montreal.

MASHA expects a kiss, but MATT barges past.

MASHA: But it isn't a mountain at all.

MATT: Back in Toronto, we walk around my neighbourhood with Nev, my French Bulldog.

MASHA: Matthew speaks to Nev in a curious manner.

MATT: You tender pooch. You nipply nugget. Nevy, Nevy, Nevy, you're such a special girl. Nevy, Nevy, Nevy, you're the specialist girl in the worrrld—

MASHA: "The specialist girl in the worrrld."

MATT: We go to the theatre, where, right before the climax of a Canadian classic, Masha memorably mutters—

MASHA: "We are surrounded by farters."

MATT: We go to "real words from real people" theatre, but Masha can't make it through.

MASHA: It's not art.

MATT: We go to a vegan restaurant, where three separate patrons scoff at Masha's fur jacket.

MASHA: A gift, from my grandmother.

MATT: We go to a jerk chicken restaurant, where three separate patrons compliment Masha's fur jacket.

MASHA: The best part about Toronto is that everyone is from somewhere else.

A moment. MASHA *dances.*

MATT: Masha is the first person I've ever met in the whole world with dance moves equally as unorthodox as my own. She is unlike anyone I have ever known.

MASHA and MATT blow a kiss to each other. A jet plane takes off. MATT is swept up by a waltz. He dances with Nev.

MASHA: After three weeks in Canada, I am in love. I have no doubt. But I'm not sure how Matthew sees our relationship in the future—or if he sees a future at all.

MATT spins.

Though, I swear he feels something serious too.

MATT: I'm falling for somebody a world away—I laugh off friends and family questioning what I'm doing pursing a relationship with someone in Ukraine.

MASHA: My experience of the "love in a distance" showed that it doesn't last. I'm not ready for another romantic epistolary episode that will last forever. I've had enough dead-end adventures.

MATT: Love conquers all.

A jet plane lands.

I return for another contract to Ukraine—just in time to see Masha perform in a night of poetry.

MASHA recites Robbie Burns.

MASHA: "But boundless oceans, roaring wide,
Between my Love and me,
They never, never can divide
My heart and soul from thee."

MATT: Masha is in full diva mode—flowers raining, champagne popping.

When we get back to Masha's flat, the diva takes her tiara off, then produces two pairs of matching Ukrainian slippers.

MASHA: Tapochki. It is important to have warm feet.

A moment.

MATT: February 1, 2020. My second contract in Ukraine involves interviewing more veterans from the ongoing conflict in the east. They repeat again and again that Russia is not done and that it is only a matter of time before Russia launches a full-scale invasion.

MASHA: I don't want to talk about war or politics—I want to discuss culture and matters of the heart!

MATT: We're talking about the suppression and erasure of culture.

MASHA: Ukraine is full of culture.

MATT: Russian culture.

MASHA: Ukrainian culture too.

MATT: How many Ukrainians can name a Ukrainian playwright?

MASHA: I'm not sure.

MATT: But they can name Russian playwrights.

MASHA: Of course.

MATT: We're the same—most Canadians can't name a Canadian playwright but since childhood have had Shakespeare drilled into them.

MASHA: You are an anti-classicalist.

MATT: I didn't know that was a thing. No, I'm against my culture, or Ukrainian culture, tacitly operating like we're inferior. Or openly! I mean, it's well documented how the British and the Russians have used their cultural canon as a colonial weapon.

MASHA throws her head back, faking deep sleep.

After swallowing Crimea, how is it still okay for the Kremlin to be funding Russian-language theatres in Ukraine?

MASHA: It is so good that you have come—now you can fix all our problems.

MATT: I'm not fixing anything. I'm just repeating what the veterans are saying.

MATT spins MASHA. Shift.

MASHA: The contract ends.

MATT: We travel to Odesa.

MASHA: So Matthew can meet my mother and father.

MATT: I've never seen drivers like the ones in Odesa. It's like every unmarked taxi is a getaway car.

MASHA: We meet my parents, divorced since I was twelve, separately.

MATT: First, we meet Masha's mother, Olga, a larger-than-life language expert.

Over Napoleon cake—which Olga and I discover we share a near spiritual affinity for—I learn that Olga grew up all over the communist world—in Cuba, Budapest, and Tambov, Russia—which I've never heard of before.

MASHA: The ancestral home of Rachmaninov.

MATT: Who I have heard of.

MASHA: The fact Matthew not only knows who Rachmaninov is, but that he had massive hands, deeply impresses my mother.

MATT: Saying goodbye to Olga, we meet Masha's father, Eugene, a doctor.

Masha informs me that she hasn't introduced a partner to her father in ten years.

MASHA: My father doesn't speak much English, but still, Matthew somehow makes him laugh.

MATT does the chicken dance.

MATT: We sit with Eugene drinking Світле пиво in a smuggler's tavern, serenaded by musicians singing about the exploits of famed Odesa bandits.

MASHA: They also sing about romance.

MATT: About smugglers stealing lovers from other smugglers.

MASHA: They have a wide repertoire.

MATT: Leaving Eugene, we walk along the shores of the Black Sea.

MASHA: My parents love you, Matthew.

MATT: Your mother says I look like Paul Giamatti and your father says that I am not an alcoholic.

MASHA: These are huge compliments!

MATT: We climb the steps of Potemkin.

MASHA: We go to the Odesa Opera Theatre, where my grandpa's soul still lives. He used to come here every week, for forty years, even when Odesa was occupied during the Second World War. We buy tickets to whatever is playing that night.

MATT: Remarkably, Khachaturian's Waltz plays to open the show—the very same waltz I danced with Nevy to, in anticipation of being reunited with Masha.

MASHA: After the performance, we sip cherry wine.

MATT: Then walk the grand promenade, in the footsteps of Shevchenko and Mark Twain.

MASHA: Dancing under the light of the moon.

MATT: To an impossibly old man with an accordion.

MASHA: Playing Céline Dion.

There is a distant echo of "The Power of Love."

О, дай мне умереть, покуда
Весь мир - как книга для меня!

MATT: Translation?

MASHA: "God, let me die right now, while the whole world is like an open book!"

MATT: See you soon?

MASHA: See you very, very soon.

MASHA and MATT dance away from each other as a jet plane takes off.

MATT: On the flight home, I sit across the aisle from a man who just can't seem to catch his breath, coughing a dry cough as we cross the Atlantic.

MASHA: Right as Matthew leaves, Covid levels in Ukraine are exploding.

MATT: Two days after we part, countries close their borders.

MASHA: The international travel ban goes into effect.

MATT: Suddenly . . . we don't know when we will see each other again.

A great division. A klezmer dirge plays.

(*to audience*) The time Masha and I spent together was incredibly special—everything felt possible. But now, a world apart, with no idea of when we'll be able to see each other again . . .

MASHA bows her head.

(*to MASHA*) We're both artists with limited means—an international romance was already a touch improbable. But now . . . the improbable's beginning to feel like the impossible.

MASHA: I try to act normally when Matthew shares his concerns, hiding my fear of losing this relationship I want so much.

MATT: Then, out of the blue, I receive a link from Masha's father, Eugene, to "Dance Me to the End of Love."

MASHA: Odesans adore Leonard Cohen.

MATT: Eugene doesn't send it with any message or explanation. Something about hearing this song makes something click. This is real.

MASHA: This is real.

MATT and MASHA stare at each other.

MATT: Not knowing when we will see each other again, I begin writing Masha every day, so I don't lose my mind.

MASHA: Red Sparrow, fly to me. Perch atop your balcony, preen your wings—then leap, and soar to the sea.

MATT: Follow the shore until you reach the mouth of the Danube, then follow it up through the Carpathians, where you will meet a Tomtit—who with, custom dictates, you must dance a hopak with.

MASHA: Cross the Danube and hug the crescent of the Alps, until you come to the Pyrenees, following the chain to the Atlantic.

MATT: Crossing the ocean, follow the route my kokom Nestichio took as a girl when her parents paddled west, until you reach Lake Win Nipee, where you will meet a Chickadee, who with, custom dictates, you must dance a Métis jig.

MASHA: Continuing, follow the Kisiskâciwan River, until you reach amiskwacîwâskahikan.

MATT: From high up, you will see a long black bridge spanning the river. You will spot me sitting atop this bridge, on the train tracks—my forehead catching the sun like a solar panel.

MASHA: Slowly weave your way down from the sky and land in front of me. Be patient. I may not recognize you right away.

MATT: When I do realize that the Red Sparrow is you, I will kiss you softly on the crown of your head, and you will transform into my Masha. And we will say—

MATT & MASHA: "Finally, we are together again."

A moment.

MATT: After a particularly poetic exchange, Masha casually informs me before I go to sleep one night that she's—

MASHA: Late.

MATT: (*still in poetic state*) Late.

MASHA: Late, late.

MATT: (*out of poetic state*) Late.

MASHA: Right.

Beat. Beat.

MATT: We agree that Masha will take a pregnancy test the next day when I'm awake and have my wits about me.

MASHA: But I can't wait.

MATT stares at MASHA.

I'm seven hours ahead—I can't wait all day!

MATT: I open my eyes the next morning to a series of emojis that inform me—

MASHA: A little squeakling is on its way.

MATT breathes.

MATT: You want to go through with the pregnancy.

MASHA: Are you joking?

MATT: No—yes, it's just, it's just something people consider, considering there's a lot to consider—

MASHA: Do you love me?

MATT: Madly.

MASHA: Then this is a blessing.

MATT breathes.

You are a reliable and responsible man. You'll be a great father.

MATT: I am not a responsible man—people told me I shouldn't even get a dog. I'm never in the same place for more than six weeks; I don't know my income from one month to the next; I've got no savings, no property.

Pause.

MASHA: That may be true. But you have been living the life of a bachelor . . . And Nevy is one of the happiest dogs I know.

MATT breathes.

MATT: I'm sorry, I'm just trying to wrap my head around everything—these are life-altering emojis I just received.

MASHA: Do you think this won't alter my life?

MATT: Of course it will.

MASHA: "My life is over, my life is over," is what I thought after I did the test.

MATT: No it's not.

MASHA: A new life is beginning—but what life? Is my career over, my dreams? My mother says she will help me raise the baby, if you do not return to Ukraine.

MATT: I will not abandon you and the baby.

MASHA: Your baby.

MATT: My baby.

MASHA: Our baby.

Pause.

MATT: Okay.

Pause.

MASHA: Will we have our baby in Odesa or in Canada?

Pause.

MATT: Well, if we have our baby in Ukraine, embassies have stopped processing passport applications, so we won't be able to legally fly to Canada with our baby—and even if I can figure out how to get into Ukraine, work won't allow me to stay indefinitely—

MASHA: Which means we would be separated again—

MATT: That's not happening.

MASHA: So, we must have our baby in Canada.

MATT: (*nodding*) But your visitor visa isn't enough to get you in anymore. Only individuals married to a Canadian national can enter.

MASHA: So . . .

MATT: So . . .

MATT and MASHA stare at each other.

I'll figure out how to fly across the world in the middle of a pandemic and sneak into Ukraine.

MASHA: I'll buy a dress.

MATT: I'll buy a tux.

MASHA: I'll book a band.

MATT: I'll pick the flowers.

MATT & MASHA: We will wed.

MASHA: Then we will travel to Canada.

MATT: Where we will welcome our squeakling.

MATT exhales.

MASHA: So, the first thing I do straightaway is study the implications of two Pisces getting married. Our union will be a blessing, or a total disaster. We are dreamers, we have rich inner worlds, but we must emerge from our heads every once in a while or we will get confused by what is and isn't real.

MATT: I need to get my life in order in a hurry. I need to find a home for my future wife, my future baby, Nevy and me. I need to be close to family.

MASHA: Packing up in Kyiv, I move back to Odesa to await Matthew's arrival.

MATT: I drive from Toronto to Edmonton. Back in Alberta, I must assuage the concerns of my mother, who is absolutely flipping out.

MASHA: My parents have met Matthew, but I have not had the opportunity to meet Matthew's parents yet.

MATT: What is giving my mom some anxiety is the double whammy that Masha and I are from different countries, and that we have only technically been dating in person for five weeks. So, we set up a virtual meeting, where I can introduce Masha to my family.

MASHA greets MATT's family, then does charades.

After a standard exchange of pleasantries and some "getting to know you" games, my mother goes from being deeply worried to liking Masha more than me by the end of charades.

MASHA: I begin to believe I will love Matthew's family . . . they are odd, like me.

MATT: Days turn into weeks, weeks turn into months . . .

MASHA: I reach the first trimester—it is so hard not to be with you right now.

MATT: How was the ultrasound?

MASHA: It's a boy.

Pause.

MATT: I thought we agreed it would be a surprise?

MASHA: During the ultrasound I closed my eyes—but my mother couldn't wait to tell me.

MATT is silent.

MATT: She shouldn't have done that.

MASHA: You're right.

MATT: I should have been there for that moment.

MASHA: But you're not here, my love. I needed her support . . .

MATT is silent.

You think I want to be with my mother at the ultrasound? You think I want to be with my mother while my belly grows?

Every day I wake up and check if Ukraine is in the green zone for travel. Every morning for eighty-nine days.

MATT is silent.

MATT: So. With the international travel ban still in effect, I take a gamble and book my flight to Odesa in one month, regardless.

My flight will take me from Edmonton to Toronto to Frankfurt to Vienna to Odesa.

MASHA: The evening Matthew gets on his flight from Edmonton to Toronto, the international travel ban is still in effect, so he is unable to check into his connecting flight to Frankfurt.

MATT: But by the time I touch down in Toronto, the international travel ban has been partially lifted.

MASHA: For the first time in four months, Canadians are now allowed into Europe.

MATT: But my connecting flight from Vienna to Odesa has now been cancelled.

MASHA: It is like the gods are tormenting us.

MATT: Not the gods, but Michael, the Air Canada ticket agent, who—while he slowly chews a chocolate-chip muffin, explains that my ticket to Europe is now void, and that there is nothing he can do about it.

MASHA: You must remain calm . . .

MATT: Come morning, I talk to a competent ticket agent, who reroutes my flight from Frankfurt to Istanbul.

MASHA: Then direct to Odesa.

MATT: I board my plane.

MASHA: Canadians are now allowed into Europe, but no one can tell us if this includes Ukraine—we have no idea if Matthew will be allowed out of the airport in Odesa, or if he will be deported upon arrival.

A jet plane takes off.

MATT: Arriving in Germany, the first Canadians to set foot in Europe nervously step forward at customs. I am permitted to catch my connecting flight to Turkey.

MASHA: Now the idea of Matthew's arrival is so real. I have horrible nausea, but I go to the airport anyway.

MATT: I touch down in Istanbul and line up for my flight to Ukraine.

MASHA: Now only a short flight away—will he recognize me, now that I look like a small hippo?

MATT: Right ahead of me, a pack of American military contractors are told they can't get on the plane—and they lose it on Turkish Airlines.

MASHA: Americans behaving badly . . .

MATT: By the time I come up with my boarding pass, the Turkish attendant is extremely flustered. Then the

Americans resume their barrage, with one of them going so
far as to threaten to fill his pants if he is not allowed on the
plane to use the toilet—so the attendant just gives me a grim
nod and lets me board.

MASHA: You are so close, my love!

MATT: On the flight to Odesa, half the Americans have
somehow managed to browbeat their way on board, so my
strategy when we touch down in Odesa is to simply be at the
back of the line again . . .

A jet plane lands.

And once again, the Americans lose it on the Ukrainian
border guards, and I stand in line for well over two hours as
they rage.

MASHA: My ankles are swollen. I have been waiting for five
hours outside arrivals—but I will not leave.

MATT: By the time I get to the border agent, I am the last
person in line. The agent says to me, "Oh, you're from
Edmonton. So is my cousin."

A stamp.

"Welcome to Ukraine."

MASHA: Matthew has been granted entry.

MATT steps forward.

But when he comes out of the airport, he's so determined to complete his mission—

MATT marches past MASHA.

—that he marches right past me!

MATT stops. He turns. MASHA raises her arms.
MATT rushes back to her.

MATT: We marry on a perfect summer morning, in the heart of Odesa.

MATT dances around the stage.

MASHA: My friends and family gather at the matrimonial hall. My bridesmaids, Alla and Alyona, fuss over the flowers in my hair. Alla is an actor, like me. A true artistic soul, very airy lady, God's dandelion. Alyona is the most reliable person I know. She is my best friend, like an arm or a leg.

Everything is ready, but, minutes before our ceremony, my groom is nowhere to be seen.

Matthew. Matt! I need you here.

MATT: I got the time wrong—everyone's always speaking in Russian.

MASHA: He was dancing in his hotel room.

MATT: I make it.

MASHA: Just in time.

MATT takes MASHA's arm. Mendelssohn's "Wedding March" plays.

MATT: I don't understand a word of the ceremony.

MASHA: I translate, when necessary.

MATT: Of the three men attending, two are named Yura. Of the six women attending our wedding, three are named Olga.

MASHA: Following Ukrainian tradition, my parents lay rushnyk linen at our feet and we step over the threshold of our new lives, together.

MATT: Continuing in tradition, we wrap our hands together with fabric, signifying being bound to each other. To do this, we use my late grammpy's Métis sash. Former clergy, I had always dreamed of my grammpy marrying my wife and I, so it is nice to feel him with us on this day.

MASHA: After the ceremony, we meet virtually with over a hundred of Matthew's friends and family. Matthew's mother cries through her speech, filled with sorrow that she cannot be with her son at his wedding.

MATT: This session is a blessing. While nobody I know is present on one of the most significant days of my life, it feels like my friends and family are with me.

The Klezmer music slowly grows as guests are introduced.

MASHA: At our wedding table, my bridesmaids get everything in order.

MATT: Alla and Alyona tell me I'm extraordinarily lucky to have a mother-in-law as kind as Olga. Without a hint of irony, Alyona informs me that the high rate of alcoholism among men in this part of the world is directly attributable to mother-in-laws.

MASHA: Ever the romantic, Alla is extremely impressed that Matthew managed to sneak into Ukraine to marry me. My father says that Matthew has Ponty, a kind of compliment usually only reserved for native Odesans. Ponty is when you are poor—when you have nothing, but you walk and talk confidently, so people believe that you are really something. My father declares that Matthew is "a hero of our time."

MATT and MASHA raise their glasses.

MATT: After dinner we dance the night away to a klezmer band that outnumbers our wedding party.

MASHA: As I had always dreamed, on the shores of the Black Sea.

MATT: Other couples who've married that same day hear that a foreigner has paid for a full klezmer band, so they show up to dance too!

MASHA: Six Odesa couples dance on the seashore as the sun sets . . .

MATT: All safely distanced.

MATT and MASHA dance. Klezmer fades.

MASHA: The night before we fly to Canada, we meet my parents for cherry wine on a cobblestone street.

MATT: Olga and Eugene's only child is now married, about to fly across the world six months pregnant, with a Canadian who's only claim to fame is that he managed to sneak into Ukraine.

MASHA: It is so hard to say goodbye to my parents and to the country that I love. We speak of when we will be together again, when we return to Odesa, when my parents will meet their grandson.

MATT: We say goodbye, not knowing when we will see Olga and Eugene again.

A jet plane takes off.

MASHA: On the flight to Canada, I am dizzy, nauseous, fighting to breathe in my mask—but I am so excited about the life that we're going to have together.

MATT and MASHA step over the threshold.

We make our nest in a little one-bedroom in Edmonton, preparing for the arrival of our squeakling.

Shift.

MATT: Before returning to Canada, we were told that Masha would be granted health care, as my spouse. But upon arrival, we learn that the authorities don't know how long her health care application will take to be processed, due to the pandemic.

If your health care doesn't come through, we'll have to pay. If we have to pay, the cost could bankrupt us.

MASHA: As soon as our baby is born, he is Canadian. But so long as he is in my womb, he is Ukrainian.

I am no one in Canada. No friends, no career, no health care . . . A zero.

I left behind my family. I left behind everything—all I have is in two bags and my belly!

MATT: You have me.

MASHA turns away. A shift.

I go to a Sweat, where prayers are sung for our son and for the health of his mom. My Elders speak about our baby in the same way Masha did when she learned we were pregnant, that our baby—our little Star Being—has chosen us.

A shift. MASHA sits with MATT.

If you're not happy here, we can return to Odesa. We came here for the passport and the health care.

MASHA: Our doula wants me to give birth in a yurt.

MATT: It would save a lot of money . . .

MASHA smiles, shaking her head.

Can you imagine the look on your father, who only agreed we should have our baby in Canada because of the health care, when we tell him his grandson was born in Alberta, in December, in a farmer's field, in a yurt?

MASHA: *(laughing)* I think he would rescind his blessing of this union, for sure.

MATT stands, helping MASHA to her feet.

MATT: Three days before Masha goes into labour, she gets health care.

MASHA: Right after my water breaks, we go to the hospital.

MATT: We get Masha into a delivery room.

MASHA: I push for five hours.

MATT: Without an epidural.

MASHA: I want the birth to be natural.

MATT: Every time Masha feels a contraction coming on, she rallies the nurses—

MASHA: "Come on, girls!"

MATT: I tell the doctor, "I'm a fainter."

MASHA: She doesn't let Matthew leave his chair.

MATT: How will we know if I'm the baby's father?

MASHA: It is better to make unsuccessful jokes than to faint right now—

MASHA cries out.

Come on, girls!

MASHA pushes.

I'm exhausted. I want to rest, but I can't. I can't stop—my body is doing it by itself. I'm out of control . . .

The baby's heart-rate monitor flutters.

MATT: Nurses and doctors flood the room.

MASHA: I push and I push, but he won't come out.

MATT: Masha, our baby is in trouble.

MASHA: *(in Russian)* Please come out, little one, please come out.

MATT: The doctor says they need to help our son come out.

MASHA nods.

MASHA: And I push!

MATT: Our baby boy doesn't cry when he is delivered—

MASHA: The nurses rush him off—

MATT: Don't get up—

MASHA: I can't hear his voice . . .

MATT: The nurses usher me over.

MATT leaves MASHA's side for the first time.

They pass me the scissors to cut the last of the umbili-cal cord.

MASHA: I hear his voice!

MASHA takes Ivan for the first time.

The nurses bring our little boy to me.

MATT: Ivan.

MASHA: Eevan.

MATT: Vanya.

MASHA: Vanichka . . .

MATT and MASHA breathe in Ivan. A shift.

MASHA: Ivan has come . . . straight from the stars. We are now two Pisces with a little Sagittarius, two water signs joined by a fire sign. He does not sleep for more than one or two hours at a time, but staring into his eyes and holding his tiny hand in mine . . .

MATT: Anyone who tells you that the first few months with a baby are amazing is probably insane.

Some moments of peace are found on walks in the river valley, where I tell him of his kokom, Kisiskâciwan, who was named after the North Saskatchewan.

Our people were some of the first in Red River, before ending up in Rosebud, Alberta.

MASHA: One year later, we have moved to Toronto. Our life has begun to feel somewhat normal.

MATT: Ivan still has trouble sleeping, but when he is awake, he is an impossibly cheery fellow. Nevy is an ever-attentive nanny, and I write a radio play about our Covid adventure.

MASHA: I make a wish for the new year: that Ivan will sleep through the night, and for our return to Ukraine. I imagine the routes we will take with Matt and Ivan, when we come to Odesa and visit my favourite places and cafés, where we

will have forschmak and then Napoleon cake. I've bought a
special sailor's suit for Ivan to enter the city in as a real little
Odesa man. And I can't wait for my dad and mom to meet
their grandson.

A shift.

On February 22, 2022, I am registered in an online acting
workshop with a group of Ukrainian actors.

Alla, my bridesmaid who is also taking the workshop, says to
me, "How good it is that you are in Canada right now . . . "

Air raid sirens rise.

February 24, 2022. Russia launches a full-scale invasion of
Ukraine. My mother messages, terrified, from Odesa—missiles have hit the port.

MATT: Our veteran friends rush to rejoin their units. Two
of the veterans—a married couple named Dima and Ira—go
to defend the Hostomel Airport outside Kyiv. Dima posts,
"Drank coffee. Brushed teeth. Waiting for tanks." Both Dima
and Ira are killed.

MASHA: Герої не вмирають.

MATT: Heroes never die.

MASHA: We try to convince my mother to get out of Odesa,
but she is too scared. I beg my father to leave—he is
sixty-seven, old enough to be allowed to leave the country.

But he refuses. He takes his duty as a doctor very seriously; he will stay and serve in Odesa, come what may.

MATT: The beach where we danced on our wedding night has been mined to guard against amphibious attack.

MASHA: The grand promenade, where we used to sip cherry wine and dance under the light of the moon, now has tank traps set up down it.

MATT: The Odesa Opera Theatre has been shuttered, with sandbags piled high in front, like Masha's grandfather would have seen during the Second World War.

MASHA & MATT: Ivan won't sleep.

MASHA: With news pouring in, we are just holding on.

We convince my mother to come, to help with her grandson.

At 4 a.m., my friend Olya, with her two children, drives my mother out of Odesa.

MATT: So that the children won't be afraid, they pretend the soldiers at the checkpoints searching for infiltrators are playing a game.

MASHA: Olya drops my mother at the Moldovan border to wait for volunteers who will drive her farther. Standing in the mud by the side of the road, she is terrified she will be robbed and murdered.

MATT: Two young men arrive, volunteers, and drive Olga to the Moldovan capital Chişinău.

MASHA: My friend Natasha lives in Chişinău and takes my mother in for two nights. But then she buses farther to Romania. All the hotels in Bucharest are full, so she must stay overnight at the airport.

MATT: She's given a yoga mat to sleep on by an airport attendant.

MASHA: In her fur coat, with five currencies stuffed in her bra, my mother lies on a yoga mat at the Bucharest airport. Like millions of Ukrainians, her life was normal two weeks before.

MATT: Flying from Bucharest to Warsaw, Olga transfers to her flight to Canada.

MASHA: The plane sits on the tarmac, the captain announcing that there has been a delay from taking off.

MATT: Olga panics—she thinks Putin is attacking Poland.

MASHA: The flight attendant calms her, assuring her they will get her to Toronto.

MATT: In the air, the woman beside Olga mutters again and again, "I did not want to leave my Ukraine."

MASHA: My mother arrives very late, so just Matthew goes to meet her.

MATT: At the airport, they're not letting people in to meet arrivals due to strict Covid rules.

MASHA: But then Matthew notices a man exiting the airport with a box of donuts . . .

MATT: Regulations state that you cannot enter the airport to meet family escaping a war zone, but you can enter the airport to buy doughnuts.

With a maple dip in hand, I go to meet Olga.

She is trembling when we embrace. She says to me, "I am so ashamed. I am so ashamed. I believed him. I believed him when he said he would not invade Ukraine."

MASHA: We reunite with my mother, crying and laughing.

Ivan's laughter can be heard.

MATT: Olga looks on Ivan like the Second Coming.

MASHA: Children are a blessing.

MATT: She feeds Ivan a shocking amount of cookies.

MASHA: And plays his favourite song again and again.

MATT: Tujamo's "Booty Bounce."

MASHA: She performs her morning exercises with Ivan.

MATT: And becomes known throughout Cabbagetown when she pushes him around, telling everyone to—

MASHA and MATT hold their fingers to their lips.

When Ivan is finally asleep.

MASHA and MATT demonstrate.

MASHA: Matt stays up late into the night to write.

MATT: Masha stays up late into the night, messaging friends fleeing Ukraine.

Shift.

MASHA: Getting my mother out of Ukraine was a huge relief.

MATT: But having Olga stay with us is not without its challenges.

MASHA: Her nickname in university was Radio because there is rarely silence when she is around.

MATT: This comes as something of a shock, as Masha is quite quiet and can happily go for hours without saying a word.

MASHA: My mother is very gregarious. She has friends all over the world.

MATT: Olga believes Ivan's car seat is a torture device—taking him out of it repeatedly while I am driving.

MASHA: Car seats were not common during Soviet times.

MATT: When I push Ivan, Olga shuffles sideways beside him, to ensure his stroller straps do not take on a life of their own and strangle him.

MASHA: My mother does not trust straps.

MATT: Olga's coup de grâce is when—after fretting because Ivan is not sleeping—she sneaks a doctor in who used to practice in the former Soviet Union.

MASHA: She should have asked permission.

MATT: The doctor determines that Ivan is perfectly fine, but declares that the high rate of anxiety among North Americans is directly attributable to our sleep-training methods.

MASHA: Many think this is true.

MATT: Olga's sleep training must have been brutal.

MASHA: She was never an anxious person before the war. Her life is now torn into "before" and "after."

Darkness begins to encroach.

MATT: Mariya. Masha. Mashenka. Matrushka. What you must be going through right now. Everyone you have ever known—their lives turned upside down.

MASHA: My father is so happy we are in Canada right now, so that we do not have to hear what he hears. His brain is misfiring—his whole life he was taught the enemy would come from the West . . . but now, they come from the East.

My bridesmaid, Alla, has stayed in Odesa. With her theatre closed, she just wanders the empty boulevards, taking selfies with stray cats and doing patriotic face-paintings. I'm afraid Alla won't last long under occupation.

My bridesmaid Alyona lives in Kyiv, but she is from Mariupol. Alyona's mother, her only family member, still lives there. The Russians block all communications, so Alyona loses contact with her. After three weeks of no word, watching on television as her hometown is destroyed, she can't take it anymore and goes to find her mother. Alyona must travel eight hundred kilometres to get to Mariupol. She passes through Ukrainian checkpoints, where soldiers can't believe she's going to a city where everyone is fleeing. Next are the invader's checkpoints. She says she has never been more scared, but they let her through. Alyona finds an abandoned bicycle on the outskirts of Mariupol. She rides through her hometown, which has been largely reduced to rubble. She takes back alleys and paths to avoid snipers and tanks, past countless bodies of civilians on the streets.

Sitting under a tree, near a bombed-out apartment building, not sure if she can go farther, a young girl emerges from below the ground with little pancakes for her . . . These give her strength. The girl gives her hope.

Alyona reaches her mother's apartment, which is somehow still intact. She opens the door and finds her mother drinking tea at the kitchen table. She grabs her mother's hand and rushes her out of Mariupol.

Everyone I have known have had their lives torn. "Before" and "after."

A shift.

MATT: We lie in bed, in our own heads now.

MASHA: Putin lies between us.

MATT: I write, trying to make sense of what is happening to our home.

MASHA: I message my friends, scattered like leaves all over the world.

MATT: I've realized, that for tax purposes, it actually benefits us to get a divorce and for you to claim refugee status.

MASHA stares at MATT.

We'd obviously remarry.

MASHA looks out.

MASHA: Matthew's jokes are reaching an intolerable level.

Ivan cries out.

MASHA & MATT: Ivan won't sleep.

MATT: Disregarding Olga's unlicensed doctor, I have convinced Masha to hire a professional sleep trainer to help us get Ivan to sleep through the night.

MASHA: But my mother is not on board.

MATT: After we have finally gotten Ivan to sleep, she sneaks into his room to put a blanket on him, waking him up.

MASHA: Mothers from Soviet times have a strong compulsion to keep babies warm. Too warm.

MATT: Olga sneaks into Ivan's room to turn off the fan—because he might go hypothermic in the night in thirty-degree heat.

MASHA: My mother does not like fans, or AC.

MATT: She sneaks into the room to disable the white-noise machine—the sound from which, she later explains, is creating pressure on Ivan's brain.

I am standing in the middle of the night in the hallway, not to make sure Ivan has fallen asleep, but to try to head off my mother-in-law.

MASHA: Matthew is very patient with her.

MATT: Until August 29, 2022, when the sleep training battle culminates at 4:30 a.m. on a Monday morning. With Ivan crying, Olga tries desperately to intervene—but I block her mad dash. She then proceeds to scream whisper through the crack in her door that I am torturing my son, that Russia employed similar methods with children in the Soviet Union—that Putin was one of these children, and that this is probably why he is insane.

Ivan finally asleep, I lie awake, seriously considering lacing the banana bread Olga is so fond of with sedative.

She is only staying temporarily.

Indefinitely.

MASHA has a nightmare.

Masha. Masha. Wake up.

MASHA: Ivan—Ivan, where's Ivan—?

MATT: He's here. He's okay. He's asleep.

MASHA: In had a dream. I was in Bucha, at a yoga retreat. And Ivan was with me. Then a bomb falls just in front of us—I grab Ivan and we run from a huge cloud of black smoke that's chasing us, and I'm scared to death, and Ivan is crying. And then I write the address of my aunt in Russia on Ivan's back. If they kill me, maybe they will at least show my baby mercy.

MATT: You need to stop reading the news in the middle of the night.

MASHA: I know. I know. But I'm so far away from my people here, it kills me.

MATT: Haunting your sleep with those images isn't helping anybody. It's not your fault you are in a safe place.

MASHA: I want to do something that's helpful. But not donations. They don't need donations. They need their homes. They need to be safe!

MATT: We can do something.

MASHA: What?

MATT: We can write.

MASHA: A play?

MATT: Yes. Write it all out—the pain, the anger, the sorrow that you're hearing about, write it all out.

MASHA: Then it will be an unending monologue about traumatized people. Nobody wants to hear that.

MATT: You experience the war through other people's stories—that's a story.

MASHA: Create a story with my friend's and family's stories?

MATT: We'll continue from where we ended the radio play.

MASHA: We'll continue.

MATT: Yes.

MASHA: Is this whole thing some sort of an adventure for you? Our marriage? Our son? The war? Is it real for you?

MATT: Of course it's real.

MASHA: When my father messages that missiles are hitting Odesa and he tells me that he is afraid for the first time in his life, and I am lying in bed praying to God to keep him safe, you are downstairs writing—pretending and playing.

MATT: I'm writing so that I don't lose my mind.

MASHA: It's an action-adventure to you. It's theoretical.

MATT: Your mother is very, very real.

MASHA: She is our guest here.

MATT: She's not a guest—she's an occupying force.

MASHA: Enough! This is my life. I am not going to transform the stories of my friends' and families' destroyed lives into art. I'm not going to be the source of inspiration for your next play.

MASHA exits. Silence.

MATT: So.

Pause.

Masha goes.

Pause.

Ivan, Olga, Nevy, and I meet her absence together. Bravely.
At first.

Ivan has always been patient with me—when his boots have
been put on the wrong feet, or when I try to get sweaters
over his sizable head . . . I feel your pain, little man. But after
three days with Masha gone, Ivan's patience comes to an end.

Not wishing to stand in the hallway, I sit on the floor in
Ivan's room . . .

He will not stop hysterically crying. So, I make the decision
to climb into his crib, to comfort him. And whether because
of shock, or because he's exhausted, he starts to laugh.
"Hahaha, Papa." To keep him on side, I tell Ivan about what
life was like before. Before Mama and Papa got together.
Before we welcomed Vanichka. Before a war on the other
side of the world turned our lives upside down . . . before life
got real.

And he is asleep.

Ever so carefully, I separate myself from him and climb out
the crib . . . catch my foot, and crash into the dresser.

"No, sweetheart, Papa didn't mean to break the lamp—
most Papas are too tall to even consider climbing into a
crib! Yes, sweetheart, Papa has a little cut and there's some

blood, which we are all full of. And yes, sweetheart, Papa is a fainter . . . "

MATT faints. MASHA in light.

MASHA: So, I go. To Niagara. I rent a little room with a view of the Falls. I buy a bottle of champagne, a pack of cigarettes . . . I sit and smoke on the balcony, trying to feel the freedom I used to have before. Before I was married. Before I gave birth. Like I am in Ukraine, before the war, young and hopeful.

She sips. She smokes.

Feel it.

She sips. She smokes.

Feel it.

She sips. She smokes.

You escaped. This is your moment . . .

She sips. She smokes.

Feel the freedom, goddamn it!

She throws the cigarette and glass off the balcony.

I book an excursion with a Ukrainian group—yeah, we're everywhere.

It is so comforting to hear my people talking, marvelling at the lights and the attractions, complaining about the weather and the cuisine . . .

We finish at the fireworks. I've always loved fireworks, and they are fantastic at the Falls.

But someone is crying. One of the girls from our group, she sits on the ground holding her knees, rocking back and forth. "She is from Mariupol," a woman of our group says. "Why has she come to see fireworks if she has just come from the war?" Maybe she just wanted to relax too, to forget, to escape. Maybe she didn't even consider she would feel under attack at Niagara Falls. Maybe she believed that she was still a normal person, another young, hopeful Ukrainian on an excursion.

No, sweetheart. Nothing is normal anymore. Nothing will be as it was before. I hold her close. The fireworks drown out her sobs. Her chest heaves against mine, her heart trying to escape so much pain . . .

Shift.

Back at the hotel I try to fall asleep. It is so quiet. And cold. No one is waiting for me. Ivan is not running up to me. My mom is not offering me some soup. Matt is not here, but I constantly talk to him in my head . . .

MATT: I regain consciousness . . . Ivan is crying . . . Olga is keening . . . Nevy is licking my wound . . . Did we get hit by a missile? No. No. We are safe. In sleepy Toronto. But Masha . . . Masha is not here.

MATT, *a moment out of time:*

An adventure . . . An adventure. Is this an adventure . . .

Pause.

Meeting Masha was a game-changer. A real TSN turning point, for sure. But we didn't know. We didn't know how it would be when we were together, after having our baby, actually . . . So I'd be lying if I said that I didn't share some of my mom's worry, that things developed a bit quickly. How could we know what we were getting into when we hardly knew who I was getting married to? So sure, I kind of turned my concerns inside out and transformed what felt like a heart attack into the spark that lit the fire of an adventure. To get to Masha. To bring her here. We jumped through hoop after hoop after flaming hoop. We were just about to buy our tickets back to Odesa . . . then the invaders poured across the border . . .

It's agonizing to watch her disappear inside herself. Trapped in this in-between place, she's not here, but she's not there. The constant jokes are an attempt to coax her back out, and yes, to cope. Talking her into writing this play was an attempt to coax her out. Because I may not have known what I was getting into when I married Masha, but I certainly know now. The way Ivan looks at her, like she is the most amazing person in the world . . . I feel you, little fellow.

I don't want what's happening over there to extinguish you here.

MASHA, *a moment out of time:*

MASHA: I didn't want to write this play.

I felt empty and torn.

All I had inside was a reflection of the war.

What can I create in this state of mind? Should I still be an artist? What for? Who needs this poetry anymore?

After all those centuries with great literature, theatre, music, "high Russian culture" . . .

Was this "high culture" so "high" that it did it not recognize the evil that had taken hold of its core? Or was this "high culture" not concerned with politics, like me, before the war?

I was so cultural . . .

But I don't want to hate. I don't want to kill.

I want to stop this war. What can I do?

If I don't have a gun, then what is my weapon? Words?

A voice.

I'm not going to be silent.

I'm not going to stuff it inside anymore.

I have to speak.

And I don't care if it's art or not.

My voice means something.

My life means something.

I'm here.

And the people who live inside of me; they are here. And their stories have value, too.

A shift. MASHA *returns to* MATT.

MASHA: Hi.

MATT: Hello.

MASHA: How are you?

MATT: Well. How are you?

MASHA: Fine. I had a nice time at the Falls.

MATT: Cigarettes and champagne?

MASHA: (*nodding*) Quite relaxing.

> MATT *and* MASHA *nod.*

I missed you terribly—I was thinking about you and Ivan the whole time.

MATT: We missed you too—Ivan refuses to sleep in his crib now—

MASHA: I thought I would feel better on my own, but I felt so empty without you two.

MATT: It wasn't fun with you gone.

MASHA: We are two Pisces—this can be amazing or go down in flames, no in-between.

MATT: We have to stay out of our brains.

MASHA: No matter what is happening in our family—

MATT: No matter what is happening geopolitically—

MASHA: We must face reality.

MATT: No more fantasies.

MASHA: No more disappearing before your eyes.

MATT takes MASHA's hands.

MATT: This is real.

MASHA: This is real. I need you.

MATT: I need you too.

They hold each other's hands. Shift.

MASHA: For my mother's sixtieth birthday, which she desperately wanted to celebrate in Ukraine, we host a small party in Cabbagetown.

After dinner we play twenty questions. When my mother is asked who her hero is, without hesitation she says, "Matthew."

MATT: I will admit, at this moment, I felt a slight twinge of guilt for considering lacing Olga's banana bread with sedative.

MASHA: Slowly, Ivan learns to sleep through the night.

MATT: We adhere to a strict routine.

MASHA: First, we read.

MATT: Then we say good night to Olga and Nevy.

MASHA: Then we blow kisses to Ukraine.

MASHA and MATT's next two lines will change, depending on the news of the day.

Today, Ukraine fights to defend her territory.

MATT: Today, Ivan is potty training and Olga and I have come to an understanding.

Shift.

MASHA: We don't know if Putin will drop a bomb.

MATT: We don't know if we are on the precipice of a world war.

MASHA: We don't know when peace will be declared.

MATT: We don't know when we will be able to bring Ivan to meet his grandfather, Eugene, in Odesa.

MASHA: But we do have hope.

MATT: We have our son.

A shift.

Dear Ivan.

MASHA: Dear Eevan.

MATT: You have been our laughing, dancing, little star through this war.

MASHA: When peace will be declared

MATT: Two small birds

MASHA: And their squeakling

MATT: Will soar.

MASHA: They will follow the Kisiskâciwan River

MATT: Until they reach Lake Win Nipee

MASHA: Where they will dance a Métis jig with a Chickadee

MATT: Then follow the river to the Hudson's Bay

MASHA: Fly across the ocean

MATT: Follow the chain of the Pyrenees

MASHA: Then the crescent of the Alps

MATT: Then the sickle of the Carpati

MASHA: Where custom dictates they must dance a hopak with a Tomtit.

MATT: Then follow the Danube.

MASHA: Until they reach the Black Sea.

MATT: And follow the shore.

MASHA: Until they come to Ukrainia.

MATT: Then, you will have come full circle, Vanichka.

MASHA: First Métis man of Odesa.

End.

Acknowledgements

The playwrights would like to thank friends, family, and colleagues who made the writing of this play possible, and to acknowledge the Ukrainian artists who have lost their lives since the launch of Russia's full-scale invasion of Ukraine.

A citizen of the Métis Nation of Alberta, Matthew MacKenzie is a multi-award-winning playwright from amiskwacîwâska-hikan (Edmonton). Artistic Director of Punctuate! Theatre, Matthew is a founding member of the Pemmican Collective and Canadian Liaison of the Liberian Dance Troupe. Matthew has had nearly a dozen of his works produced across Turtle Island.

Ukrainian actor and playwright Mariya Khomutova started her theatre studies in Odesa at the age of twelve. She graduated from the Kyiv National Theatre University in 2012 and worked in two repertoire theatres in Kyiv before moving to Canada in 2020. After February 24, 2022, Mariya concentrates her theatre work around promoting contemporary Ukrainian playwrights' voices to the world theatre community.

First edition: September 2024
Printed and bound in Canada by Imprimerie Gauvin Ltée., Gatineau

Jacket art and design by Gracia Lam
Author photos by Alexis McKeown

Playwrights Canada Press
202-269 Richmond St. W., Toronto, ON M5V 1X1
416.703.0013 | info@playwrightscanada.com | www.playwrightscanada.com

Support Ukraine